The Monitor and Laughter of the Gods
Saraswati Comes Swingin' Her Hips

The Monitor and Laughter of the Gods
Saraswati Comes Swingin' Her Hips

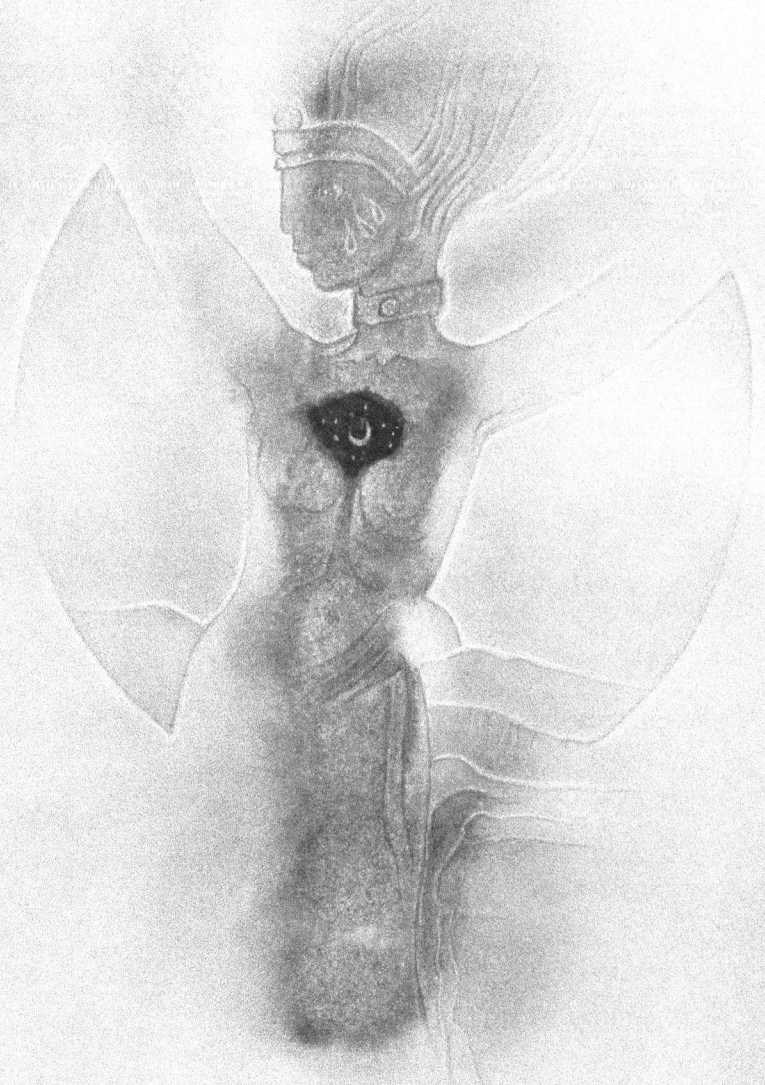

Mary Saint-Marie
Sheoekah Amu

© 2013 Mary Saint-Marie / Sheoekah. All Rights Reserved.

No part of this book may be reproduced, stored in a retrieval system, or transmitted by any means without the written permission of the author.

Published by Ancient Beauty Studio, www.marysaintmarie.com

ISBN: 978-0-9646572-1-2 (sc)

All artwork by Mary Saint-Marie

Cover Art: *Sacred Dancer of Life-SHE...*

> *the light does dance...*
> *galactic stars revealing ever...*
> *the world is within...*

Book Design and Layout by Aaron Rose, Mount Shasta, California

Other publications by Mary Saint-Marie:
Galactic Shamanism
The Holy Sight
Messages from the Silence
Nectar of Woman
The Sacred Two
The Star-Stone Ones
The Animating Presence

Dedication

The Monitor and Laughter of the Gods
is dedicated to
the ecstatic watcher/seer in us all.

Contents

Acknowledgments 9

Introduction 13

Preface 15

A Sacred Enactment 17

The Monitor and Laughter of the Gods 23

The Monitor as a Messenger of Balance 75

The Two Men as World Catalysts 77

The Essence of Saraswati 79

The World of Shanti, Joy, and The Wise Woman 81

The World Home 83

Soul Responses to the Play 85

About the Artist/Writer 89

Paintings, Art Exhibits, Soul Sessions,
The Holy Sight Workshops, Books, and CDs 93

Additional Plays or a Documentary 95

Acknowledgments

I thank my beautiful daughters, Kimberly Backes and Rebecca Allen, for being in my life. I am touched by whatever form that does take.

I am in gratitude for Kelly Hunnewell, who saw so clearly the play in book form and prompted me to publish. The prompting worked. And here it is, Kelly.

I am thankful to Laura Daen for uplifting encouragement to create the book form. Always a joyful muse!

I am deeply grateful to Heidi Merkins for supporting the manifestation both of the play and the shift into book form. I feel your presence in it all, Heidi.

I am thankful for Aaron Rose for the book and cover design. Aaron makes it all seem so easy. He attunes to the soul of the book and weaves enlightened designs. It is like play to create together.

With such deep appreciation I thank the Christed Presence that lights my way in the manifestation of *The Monitor and Laughter of the Gods,* first as an original play in theatre form and now as a book.

....

Listed below are also acknowledgments for the original play production on stage in August of 2011, in Ashland, Oregon. The play's existence was the first incarnation: it also helped to inspire this book form.

All of the ones below were part of the alchemy that now brings forth the book form.

I give deep appreciation for the collaboration with so many creative people. (This was my first play, so I was just a beginner, learning every moment. I did not know that it would lead later to a book.)

I thank Laura Daen for playing the role as muse, giving welcomed insights about the manifestation of *The Monitor and Laughter of the Gods* as an original play from its inception.

I thank Heidi Merkins and Donna Jackson for making this play a reality on stage in Ashland, Oregon in August, 2011. Your presence throughout was felt.

I am in deep appreciation for the large number of gifted and experienced ones who brought the play to ecstatic life on the stage and ones who worked tirelessly with their talents offstage. I hesitate to give a list of names, in concern that someone might be overlooked. (There are some volunteers whose names are not included, such as the man who provided such awesome cookies at the break.)

Directors: Peter Alzado of Oregon Stage Works and Mette Kolding

Producers: Kate Sullivan and Mary Saint-Marie

Actors and Dancers: Kate Sullivan, Dennis Nicomede, Michael Meyer, Mette Kolding, Sahadev Pool, Laura Daen, Graell Corsini

Musicians: Sahadev Pool, Dawn Fazende and sacred chanters, Prakriti Das

Assistant Director: Bill Ritch

Lighting Design and Technician: Mark Ursetta

Sound Design: Sahadev Pool

Special Effects: Sahadev Pool

Choreography: Laura Daen

Photography and Tickets: Joi Shannon Photography

Poster and Program Design: LightSource Creations, Medford, Oregon

Box Office: Susan Wolcott

Production Assistant: Donna Rae Swartwood

Music Composition: Sahadev Pool

Music: Courtesy of World Meditation Ensemble and Omega Organization International

Camera Man: Paula Rudy

Theatre: CultureWorks Café and Performing Arts Center, Ashland, Oregon

Ticket Sponsors: The Gallery of Mount Shasta and The Music Coop in Ashland

I thank you ALL!

And…I am in full gratitude for the conscious audience each night of the performance.

Their "viewing" brought the play to life on stage in a heightened way. They were an awake audience who mirrored the play with lively responses. They were in full participation. A play is not fully a play without the aware audience. They were a reflection in a lucid pond.

I am also in appreciation for the many that wrote or called in their responses to the play. And I thank also the ones that stopped me on the street to exclaim the ways they were affected by the words of the theatre production.

I thank, Roberta Ossana, editor of *Dream Network Journal,* who published an article about the play in the Spring 2012 issue of the magazine.

Introduction

An actor enquired of me, upon reading *The Monitor and Laughter of the Gods,* if I was a playwright. I was silent. All I could voice was that I had written what was before them. It simply arrived. Uninvited. I fully welcomed it as an unexpected and radiant guest. I embraced it upon arrival.

For two days I entertained the guest. Or should I say…it entertained me. Then it stopped.

The guest filled my two days in solitude, in retreat.

The inner communing had an uplifting and exalting effect on me. I seemed to be in another world, yet fully in this one. I found myself laughing out loud as the stream of consciousness came forth. A profound experience of the natural and supernatural as one.

I found myself aware of the world in a way that was a simple noticing. I could see the world in its mis-creations that create endless fear, pain, and suffering, without reacting. Yet that does not mean there will not be a response and action.

In the inner communing, we find ourselves simply Being. We find ourselves at One with the Animating Presence. We find ourselves to be Action borne of Vision rather than action borne of reaction. We find that this type of Action has a different effect in the world. It is not a perpetuation of opposition, battle, and warring consciousness. It is not fueling the combat stance. Rather, it can create in the world from a transcendent and transparent Consciousness.

I offer *The Monitor and Laughter of the Gods: Saraswati Comes Swingin' Her Hips* as a guest in your life. It is a reminder of "being in the world, but not of it." It is a reminder of staying in, abiding in the Animating Presence. It is a reminder to Allow Life to be revealed. It is the numinous awareness that we may all live from this ever expanded Awareness.

Enjoy the guest.

Preface

The Monitor and Laughter of the Gods generates a surreal, mystical and humorous meeting of consciousness with Consciousness. It befriends Truth in an unexpected and irreverent context. It reminds us all starkly and directly that all of humanity is on notice to go beyond the realm of beliefs and touch the wordless and nameless one that dissolves boundaries between races, religions, traditions, countries, and seeming separations everywhere.

The Monitor and Laughter of the Gods is revealed as the silent, ecstatic witness, watcher, observer, seer in us all. In that, Inspiration is seen as the inner one where the mystery of the Unknown becomes the Known.

One revels in naked delight as Saraswati continues to remove the veils of separation. As original archetypal woman does she dance the One Dance of Balance. As Goddess of Reciprocity does she swing her hips in the rhythm of the Earth, reminding us of Home.

Ever will ones be uplifted in the exaltation of the realm of the real.

A Sacred Enactment

The writing of the stream of consciousness play, *The Monitor and Laughter of the Gods,* came forth with no planning, no intention. I can only say that I was utterly surprised in the present moment, yet receptive. The entire unfoldment was a seeing of the ordinary and the extraordinary as one. The dreaming and the waking as one. I felt more like a witness to its coming, yet paradoxically I was seeming to be "in" it as well.

It began in this way.

It was October, 2008. I felt a deep need for solitude. I chose October 18th and 19th as my days of inner reflection. I was on retreat.

I had no intuitions about how I would spend time on the retreat. I spent those days writing—morning, noon, and night. I was not trying to write a play, nor any genre whatsoever. I was simply writing what was there in consciousness. At times I could both be aware of the words to write and sometimes see or sense the entire scene on the inner planes of sight. And I could feel the tone that rendered clear the meaning.

What happened was that dreaming and waking appeared in my world as one and the same. The following lines, taken directly from the play, describe the initial experience best.

"Much information is passed back and forth which I cannot seem to remember because I am waking up. I am lying in bed. It is morning. I was dreaming.

For a flash, I remember my prayer before I went into meditation the evening before. I asked within, like never before, that my sleep, dreams, and waking states all be in the One Consciousness.

I said, 'I am tired of lapsing into unconsciousness. I want to be Awake and lucid all the time.' I said that to myself, meditated, and went to sleep.

I struggle a moment to stay in the dream. I know it is important. I relax into that between-wake-and-dream zone of early mornings, that dawn period that I love. It is the place where rapture dwells, exaltation even. It is the Place that is not a place, where I get revelations, ideas, contacts. Some call it God. Some… Presence. I heard it call Itself "I AM" once. But It said it without words and without a voice. It is indeed marvelous to hear the Unspeakable Speak.

I am back in the dream. And I am awake. I am in charge. I can stop the dream or keep it going. I don't want to stop it. Answers, Awareness seem to fill the space."

From that aware space, with inner listening and sometimes seeing, the writing continued. For two days it continued. I prepared meals. I sat joyfully in the sun on the deck. I walked and gazed at the mountain and lake. I was quiet in the evenings. And still the words continued to pour in. Sometimes it was very subtle. It could have been easily missed had I not been ultra-open and listening on retreat. I carried pad and pen everywhere. It was a new writing experience, since the dream-awake was alive in me for two days. Then the words stopped, as abruptly as they started. The energy of the two days was heightened. I was ecstatic.

The writing was a Living Vision and I was a participant, residing somehow in it all.

The Dream. The Awakeness. The mystical zone that joined them.

Ten weeks after writing the dream-awake experience, I wrote a description of what appeared to be a play to send to a friend.

"The Monitor generates a surreal, mystical and humorous meeting of the consciousness with Consciousness. It befriends Truth shared in an unexpected and irreverent context. It reminds us all starkly and directly that all of humanity is on notice to go beyond the realm of beliefs and touch the wordless and nameless one that dissolves boundaries between races, religions, traditions, countries, and seeming separations everywhere.

The Monitor is revealed as the silent, ecstatic witness, watcher, observer, seer in us all. In that, Inspiration is seen as the inner one where the mystery of the Unknown becomes the Known.

One revels in naked delight as Saraswati continues to remove the veils of separation. As original archetypal woman does she dance the One Dance of Balance. As Goddess of Reciprocity does she swing her hips in the rhythm of the Earth reminding us of Home.

Ever will the audience be uplifted in the exaltation of the realm of the real."

The friend who had already read the play wrote:
"It is the Awakened inviting the asleep.
 Seduction…in its truest sense,
 A Play of Cosmos into form.
 The formless dances upon the stage
   with simple sweet seductive satisfaction
    baring deep-seeded Fear's Farce.
 Calling the emperor naked."

The Monitor and Laughter of the Gods is very simply a chronicled journey and conscious communing between the awake and the awakening.

The communication takes the form of a woman, who goes by the name The Monitor, who is questioned by two men who find her intriguing and strange in her ways. They are curious and end up asking piercing questions about the universal perspective of life. The Monitor questions whether she has created them or whether they have created her. The humor continues throughout as The Monitor reveals the Oneness that they are.

The Monitor represents all of humanity's nobility.
The Monitor portrays Awareness. She represents the no-mind, the indigenous mind.
The Monitor reveals the Mystical as the Practical in us all.
The Monitor embodies the archetypal force of the divine feminine principle.
The Monitor is a messenger for the universal law of balance.
The Monitor sees and reports.

These two men represent us all. Everyman. They are awakening out of their old condescending attitudes toward the universal feminine values. They are awakening out of the linear, left brain world of seeming separation. They are awakening out of beliefs. They are between the two paradigms and are "messengers" for those still stuck in seeming separation and the ensuing fear. They are in a deep observing stage with the "strange" woman. There is a genuine disbelief and curiosity, but no disdain or mockery.

These two men are attracted to the new Consciousness. They like what they see. They see mirrored their own true nature.

The two men are very important. They represent the unfolding new culture. They embody the unfolding receptive nature in us all.

The sacred enactment is filled with music and chanting by a universal man named Shanti who represents love that has no conditions. Dancing and playfulness fills the space by his friend, Joy, who comes and goes, bringing light-heartedness in her wake.

Saraswati, the Universal Goddess of Balance, slows the pace to a profound entry into the rhythms of the music borne of the Infinite. The Great Mystery penetrated. Perceived. The Mystical dancing in form! Beauty in motion.

And there are two moments that make it look as if the Chorus of the ancient Greek plays is returned unto this time of grand awakening. Wise Woman does step onto the stage adorned in cape and staff, holding space for the Law of Balance to be recognized, honored, and realized.

Following the play are five chapters that are available as the writer's response to the experience as it was coming through.

The chapters are optional and not intended to direct the experience of the reader, much like an artist speaking about their own painting.

These chapters may also be read before reading the play, as a way to connect with the essence of the material.

The Monitor and Laughter of the Gods

I am with a man, Shanti, who is with a woman, Joy. Joy comes and goes. Shanti and I meet up here and there. I am traveling. Shanti and I are meeting now with two men who are extremely interested in what we are doing and what our lives are about. As one of the men starts talking to me, I can feel this increasing energy between my eyebrows. It is growing and is very strong. It seems to be opening up my ability to know and see clearly. To know outside of the realm referred to as ordinary.

Much information is passed back and forth which I cannot seem to remember because I am waking up. I am lying in bed. It is morning. I was dreaming.

For a flash I remember my prayer before I went into meditation the evening before. I asked within, like never before, that my sleep, dreams, and waking states all be in the One Consciousness. I said, "I am tired of lapsing into unconsciousness. I want to be Awake and lucid all the time." I said that to myself, meditated, and went to sleep.

I struggle a moment to stay in the dream. I know it is important. I relax into that between-wake-and-dream zone of early mornings, that dawn period that I love. It is the place where rapture dwells, exaltation even. It is the Place, that is not a place, where I get revelations, ideas, contacts. Some call it God. Some…Presence. I heard It call Itself "I AM" once.

But It said it without words and without a voice. It is indeed marvelous to hear the Unspeakable Speak.

I am back in the dream. And I am awake. I am in charge. I can stop the dream or keep it going. I don't want to stop it. Answers, Awareness seems to fill the space.

The two men are questioning me. Shanti sits nearby in Silence.

....

The Monitor:
Why are you here? *(on planet Earth)* I hear the men say.

The Monitor:
I am a Monitor.

Man:
What are you monitoring?

The Monitor:
I am monitoring the planet.

Man:
How do you do that?

The Monitor:
It is something I have always done.

Man:
Where did you learn to do that?

The Monitor:
I must have learned it in class before I was born. And

those are only words to try to give you understanding prior to what is called birth.

Man:
What are your earliest memories of monitoring?

The Monitor:
From age one through three years I monitored my surroundings, staying in the sweetest love. (My mother described it all to me one day.) Then something happened. My love for my mother pulled me away from that Place. I saw her so sad and in so much pain. I let my heart follow her into the world where she lived. And just like that, I found myself in her world. Emotional, dizzying, and fright-filled. I wanted to save my precious mother from the tortures and agonies that were her life. I began to use my monitoring gift to track my mother. I did not know then at that young and innocent age of between 3–4 years that I had entered the hell realm of humanity's creation. Metaphysicians would call it the astral realm. I did not know that I might forget the innocence and the purity of the Place of sweetest love where all is always harmony. I took all that love and directed it at my sweetest mom. She was diminutive. Only five feet, one inch. I found that I was feeling something I had no words for. Hate and rage and fear is what I later learned they were. The violence on my mother was from my dad.

I would get so lost in this hell realm of emotions that I would pray each night for my dad to die in a plane crash. He was a pilot, as was my mom. I knew it was not good to pray for that. I just could not think of anything else to save my mother. I don't want to discuss the nature of the ongoing violence. It has no purpose now.

Man:
How did you ever get out of this? You were young.

The Monitor:
Between three and four, I found Nature. I found the outdoors. Nobody ever seemed to know where I was or what I was doing or even when I came and went. One of my favorite things to do was climb trees. I sat as high in the branches as I could get. Sometimes it was in fruit and nut trees and I could eat. I loved that. Other times I was quiet and empty in my own sweet world, the Place. I loved that. I made friends with squirrels. On an island we owned, I made friends with crabs, who showed me their lives and would let me get as close as I wanted. I told them I would never harm them or even scare them. I remember getting to ride on the back of a great sea turtle. One night and then nights, I was served sea turtle soup with peas and tomatoes to eat. My sadness knew no end. And I took care of birds I would find…with broken wings. I fed them bread soaked in milk until one day they would fly away. When I wanted candy, I would get a tablespoon from the kitchen drawer and go to my secret space under a bush, next to my grandfather's great Victorian home, where our family also lived at that time. There I would dig up coins to spend. I never questioned how the money got there nor even how I knew it was there.

Nature came to be my friend, my best companion, my comforter, my provider. In Nature, I began to find my way. I could leave this "hell world" and be easily in the world of the innocent love. It was the Place where it "feels good." I saw that high in the trees I could leave this world of horror and terror that was below.

Man:
Speak more about monitoring.

The Monitor:
When innocent eyes can fall upon this hell world, it begins to shift, to reorganize. You would call it the single eye, the third eye, God, or something else. It is pure Consciousness. It is like a soothing balm. It cannot pretend anymore. It cannot get away with lies. It does not want to lie.

Man:
Then why did not your gaze help your mother?

The Monitor:
In part, it did; I became great solace for her. But when I made the mistake of following her into the hell realm, I was sucked into that and would Fall into a seeming separation from the innocence and purity of that inner Place. I could then only get clear of it in Nature or deep in the night.

Man:
How does this translate into your life now? Are you still a monitor?

The Monitor:
Every day I seem to wake up more. Revelations are not of

scripture only. They are our Awareness. I can often now easily and accurately see how to guide situations, from individual conflicts to huge global dramas, back into the harmony of What Is. For What Is…is harmony.

Man:
What about the unending battle of light and dark?

The Monitor:
That is all an epic pretending of battle. A drama of duality. Everyone that is a part of it has at some point bought in for their own personal mental belief. As a child, I did it to save my mother. Everyone thinks they have a good reason. Reason is mental, made up in the ever-scheming human mind of beliefs.

....

As I lie in bed observing this fascinating and curious dialogue between me and these two men, I realize I am somewhere between dreaming and waking still. I am in a zone of awareness that makes no distinction between dream and awake. I can even be closer to the dream or closer to the awake state, at will. When I am closer to the dream, I am concerned that I will forget what I am dreaming. When I am closer to the awake state, I am concerned that beliefs will disconnect me from this steady stream-of-consciousness that is pouring in.

I find that I can adjust awareness, so that I am just in between. A little like Goldilocks when she says, "This is just right."

As I lie in bed, I realize the insights could still be put in the context of questions and answers from the men or I could just let insights come. It is just that questions bring a focus.

....

Man:
We are still here wanting to know more. Why have you lived as an artist for so many years?

The Monitor:
Painting the inner realms of purity has afforded me a way to stay in Presence and access that Consciousness, reachable by all. It is much like climbing trees as a child.

Man:
Speak more about what it means to be here on the planet as a monitor.

The Monitor:
Well, first of all, function as a monitor is not a career. One cannot go to a university to learn to function in this way. It is all about living in Consciousness. Please make the distinction between human consciousness (lives lived in seeming separation, as if there had been a Fall) and Consciousness.

The word monitor is a rather worldly way to describe "seeing through the eyes of purity."

Man:
Why then do you wear glasses?

The Monitor:
I still carry some residue of my own seeming Fall. At age

twelve, and I remember the entire drama, I chose to not see well for reading. It seemed to me that I was protecting myself from this world that had no heart. I can see what it will take to not wear them again, but I am not ready for that leap.

Man:
Okay, back to you as a monitor.

The Monitor:
I am not a monitor, in the sense that I identify with that function. It is simply what I do from that land of purity. Anyone can learn to do it.

Man:
You realize, don't you, that the world frowns on purity. It conjures up thoughts of the belief in some sort of Perfection.

The Monitor:
I am keenly aware of that. It is simply another way that the world gives itself more imagined time in this make-believe realm of good and bad. There is so much investment in money, time, study, preparation, identity that the human mind cannot afford it. Even if they wanted to, there would be a possible bigger global economic collapse. Those that are already awake or are awakening are finding ways to step out of the drama. It has been happening one person at a time. They are forming groups, clans, communities, villages. Even conscious ones in cities are leading the way. They might not call it The Purity Revolution, but that is what it is. Think about it. The natural and organic movement from

the 60s saw a higher ideal; they saw living in harmony with Nature. Many were people of vision. They were before their time. They did not have all the answers, but the movement was initiated.

Man:
And the word purity? How can that be introduced without negative attitudes like purist, goodie-goodie, impractical dreamer, and on?

The Monitor:
This awakening that is happening worldwide is a breaking though of Pure Consciousness. What appears to be human consciousness can fall away. This seeming human consciousness is little more than Divine Consciousness covered with one or many beliefs. These beliefs show up in the form of opinions, judgments, interpretations, preferences. These in turn cause a distortion, a perversion, or a simple misinterpretation of the "fact of Purity." It is that simple.

Man:
What is the solution?

The Monitor:
Ha, well in human terms we would say that a good brand of window cleaner would be good. We don't mind clean windows. Yet we allow the window of the mind, which is the Mind, to become clouded, fogged, and hazy to varying degrees. We have chosen the path of beliefs. The solution is "transparent Mind." People are awakening to the non-dual world.

Man:
Is there a class, workshop, or book that will help to find pure, transparent Mind again?

The Monitor:
That is the problem. People look for a giant eraser in the form of some person outside of themSelves. That can help if the teacher is authentic. For that, one needs discernment. Ultimately, one must do a very simple thing. Desire, in one's own way, Realization of the One Self. That attention will open new experiences and insights and direction.

Man:
That is way too easy. No one will believe that.

The Monitor:
Yes, that is why the awakening is happening at the current pace. It is Perfect. Word is passing from person to person. Spiritual prejudice is being exposed worldwide, as the exclusivity that it has embraced, lived, and promulgated far and wide, causing endless war that has created in turn this seeming hell realm. Truly it is Perfection seen with the "blinders of belief."

Man:
Are you saying that this is a spiritual universe and it is just that no one notices or wants to notice?

The Monitor:
I am. Change is hard for those with resistance. In fact, it is painful. There is so much investment in the false beliefs.

Man:
No one is going to believe this!

The Monitor:
I am not asking for anyone to believe anything. I am simply monitoring. I am holding space, the best I can, in the Realm of the Real. That is all I need to do.

Man:
How do you know that "just gazing in a certain way" can bring change?

The Monitor:
In my deep asking for Truth, for knowing of my True Self, I was granted two experiences many years ago. I thought at first that I was being delivered into the astral hell. Only as I followed the inner bidding did I realize I was being initiated into a deeper understanding of Purity. Call it what you would like. Buddha Mind. Christ Mind. Divine Mind. All the same, once one opens beyond the differentiated paths to what might be called Pathless Path.

Here is what happened. I was meditating. My inner eye had been open for years, revealing glory after glory. (Those would be too long to explain right now, other than to say that glorious is what exists beyond the hell realms created by the clever conditioned human mind.) This time I saw into the astral realm. The diabolic images revealed seemed like a composite of the most horrific world the mind could ever conjure. Even the slightest gazing upon these pictures that seemed so real, caused great forgetfulness, slumber, and fear. I could barely remember to open my eyes to be free of the images. As I opened my eyes, I was stunned and frightened. I prayed to know why this was happening. I was simply meditating as I always had, in Christ Presence.

Here is what I was guided to do: Close my eyes, keeping a strong focus on the Light of the Living Christ that I am. O hey, that is the Purity that so many are fearing. Oops, the opposite is what we should be fearful of, if there is going to be fear. Hmmmm, how did we ever get it backwards? We have been falling straight into the misuse of the mind. What a movie. And it is ever only a movie. We have been living the make-believe of a child and pretending that it is real. And now we wake up in the movie, wondering how to get out.

Maybe we become Theseus and the Minotaur story of following the ball of thread out of the labyrinth of the monster. That is our story. That is our awakening. It is a delight and surprise for all to find out that the seeming Fall and the seeming separation was not free. There has been a price to pay. That price is our joy, our freedom, and liberation.

Back to the meditation. I entered the "astral hell" being revealed in the third eye. I entered identified as the Light. This has to be where the word Behold came from. Lo and Behold. Or even Wow! I watched, under the steady gaze of the Christ Light, the images of hell shapeshift into that which I can only describe as Unspeakable Beauty. The Soul's majestic expression. Even the quantum physicists are teaching now that we affect everything that we gaze upon. I witnessed and observed and experienced Transcendence in form. I witnessed what together we can do, what we came to do. That is to experience our Oneness. To experience formed and formless as One. To experience that we Already live in a Spiritual Universe.

Man:
Do you believe that people in the world will actually believe this? Do you believe that they will listen to you and others?

The Monitor:
It really does not matter what anyone believes. Once you have experienced yourself as the OneSelf, you are no longer interested in engaging in beliefs. One who monitors holds space in Awareness, with no thought, and acts as a Vision Keeper. When one has seen the hilarity of this human act, one realizes we are in the throes of agony on this planet because we chose it. It would be worth conjuring up images here of the Laughter of the Gods. Cosmic joke. Until ones start to question their beliefs they will be stuck, to a certain degree, in the movie. It could even make them angry to think of an image like the Laughing Buddha. This anger could be the jolt that opens them up. Whatever is the jolt, the disease, the accident, the opponent that wakes them up, then somehow it is their time. It must be noticed by now that the collective jolts are increasing worldwide. The electronic communication is allowing global monitoring. The 911 was not the towers of the USA alone. The 911 is the call for help. It is that call for help that wakes us up out of the

dream, this movie of hell. Pain and loss and fear receive strong attention.

Man:
So what is real here, the dream, with us asking you questions, or you waking up and making up our questions?

The Monitor:
(Laughter) Now you are more fun! You are bringing in the Laughter of the Gods. This entire movie is the Light shining on our beliefs and BAM, just like in the comics, it is so. Kind of like a Presto! *(Laughter)*

Now imagine this! Imagine the world taking no thought. Just the Light of Presence impulsing, envisioning, enacting directly through these vehicles we call bodies.

Now imagine this! No limitation! No limitations at all. Then…it is…that Glory makes her collective appearance. She has been waiting. She has been waiting in the wings. She is the wings and she takes flight upon our remembering, our recognition of what is, our realization of Oneness. "I and the Father are one" was not just about Jesus. It is literal. I and God are One. This is true for all.

Man:
Blasphemy. That has been called blasphemy.

The Monitor:
It is much too late in the movie for such words. The Reality Is! Such words have created spells to control the masses through the ages. Hey, groups of people could

get together and find the rest of the words with that mal-intent to cover truth. Better than Monopoly. In fact, Monopoly is of the old. Find new games for yourselves in this Theseus myth.

....

I get out of bed at noon. I have been writing all morning. People eat. I need to eat. A belief! We can all have fun with that one. Of course, there are already people living without eating.

As I sit on the deck loving the sun and silence, I realize that this is "the experience" of dream, waking, and the zone in between, as one. Then I "hear" the men asking another question.

I wonder, are the men in the dream part of my own imagination to help me, via dream, to create greater Awareness of my own part here on the planet? Or are these two men from another realm serving me as guides to a more luminous life along the way? You know, this is what I can handle, so allow two strangers to drag answers out of me. Or maybe neither. Something greater! Vaster. Or just a dream in alchemy with my waking state?

....

Man:
Hey there, what is the answer to all this?

The Monitor:
I will leave it to the individual to answer. Ask me this question: How can we know and be certain of answers?

The mind is so clever.

Man:
Okay, let that be our question.

The Monitor:
Get ready for an answer so simple as to be ignored, forgotten, laughed at, and hey, even sneered at and mocked at by some through the ages.

Man:
We are ready.

The Monitor:
FEEL

Man:
That is silly. That is the bodily senses.

The Monitor:
Feel deeper.
Feel with your Soul.
Feel with the Presence that you are.

Man:
Is this a trick? How does one do that?

The Monitor:
Realize yourself as Consciousness.
Identify with Consciousness.
Again make sure you make the distinction between consciousness and Consciousness.
The second one takes no thought.
The first one is lost daily in many thoughts.

Man:
What then?

The Monitor:
After a while one discovers that one can actually "feel" Presence. Feel the Light. This causes great disarmament. Looking at the human miscreations reminds one of looking at a mirage while driving across a desert. As you get closer to it, it disappears. It is not real. It never was real. It is an illusion. Sure did look real.

Well, friends, we have many mirages to notice. We have all been Don Quixote, battling windmills of the mind.

Man:
There is going to be much resistance to such notions.

The Monitor:
This is not a notion. And as to the resistance, it is only from those who believe that they have something to lose or maybe even gain. They will battle on, creating war after war in their psyche, looking for ways to externalize it.

Man:
Will they ever stop?

The Monitor:
When the suffering is great enough or when there is a catastrophe or disaster. OR, and this is important, when enough people have stepped out of the movie. When enough people are not feeding and fueling that dream of miscreation, it will burst like a balloon. Deflate. Poof! Enter center stage…non-duality!

Man:
Here is the big question: Will life be fun anymore? Will life be exciting anymore? Conflict is what keeps it interesting.

The Monitor:
(*Laughter*) What do you mean? Life will finally be fun!

Man:
It sounds like there will be all harmony. As boring as a never-ending waltz. Where is the passion and the heroes? Where is the action?

The Monitor:
Humanity mistakes the idea of passion with conflict. Being a knight as a Lancelot, equipped with blazing lance, going off to fight the battle of good and evil for his lady. Humanity has endlessly lived this out. The hero, and occasionally a heroine, has the bravado to "kill evil."

Those are great stories that reveal the epic battles of brutality and savagery through the ages. But what about "and they lived in peace ever after?" Who has written that story? Who has asked the question? Who wants to ask the question? Who will listen? Through the ages we forgot to ask the question of what is the "peace ever after" story. Does anyone want to know?

Man:
What a notion! What does peace look like? What is that story?

The Monitor:
It is not a notion. Peace is the "what's next." Peace is fun.

Peace is where Glory enters on stage.

Man:
We want to have a sneak preview. Just a few glimpses. We will decide for ourselves.

………………………………

An image is seen. In front of these men walks a woman of great knowing. She is an elder. Striking. Hair and scarves are blowing in the wind. The men wipe their eyes to see if they are seeing things. The wind seems to blow through this woman as she steps through the garden wall where they sit, almost shaking now.

………………………………

Man:
Was that the devil? Doing tricks? Was that a ghost of the Inquisition? Whoa! We thought you said this would get fun.

The Monitor:
(Laughter) It is fun. You observed a quite natural gift of man/woman to expand their cells a little and be the energy body that they are. THAT is fun! Playing in the field of formed and formless as One. Perhaps read more quantum physics. Talk to the ones who have had visitations from other realms. See that all is Energy. And your world will change.

To live in the world you just glimpsed, you must take your attention off the seduction of the dire drama of duality. Perfection is a fact. Purity is a fact. And because it is an inviolate and established fact, everyone has the good fortune of becoming a master of Energy. Everyone has the good fortune of being the scientist so well as to have the experiment become the living proof.

Man:
That did look fun. Are there any catches?

The Monitor:
There IS one thing you need to know. But it is not a catch. The inexorable principle of Love is the law of the One. We are all One.

Man:
What does that have to do with walking through a wall?

The Monitor:
All thoughts, words, actions must be for the good of the Whole. For the good of the One. The One that we already are. This principle of One works through us and AS us, as we allow. We do not personally use it. In that we fail. And suffering returns.

Man:
Give an illustration.

The Monitor:
The picture I offer is this: Should you walk through a wall in order to hurt another, for your own personal, selfish greed, you will be violating the law. We are all the One Self. So Self giving to Self. That is the Balance. That is the Love. This is an Impersonal Life.

Man:
So this is a trick! To know how to do that, we must follow

rules and regulations. This is not freedom. That sounds like slavery. That sounds like being a puppet.

The Monitor:
You can learn how to do this and misuse it for personal gain if you wish. That is up to you. Do not mistake that for freedom. Yes, it is true, you would be freely living what you believe to be freedom. That you can do. And there are consequences. You are confusing a seeming act of choice and free will for freedom.

True freedom is living from your true Self. You are acting like yourSelf can't do what it wants. Rather, yourself, aligned with the Whole, will do and receive all that is ever dreamed of and more. It is the human self, cut off from Source, its True Self, that is lost, confused, confounded. It can be seduced, allured by almost everything. It has dulled its Awareness. Anything with sparkle, sheen, or shine attracts. That is how Hollywood became so popular. It gives the seduction and promise of power and money and excitement. We have now woven that into many governments. One does need compassion here. Do you know how dull an 8-to-5 office job can be? I hear stories.

Man:
Did we hear you right? God is ourself or our Self, as the case seems to be. Is this our joy? And our freedom?

The Monitor:
That is what I am communicating.

Man:
Whoaaa! How long will that take?

The Monitor:
There you go again! Fascinated with Time. In truth, it will take you as long as you would like. *(Laughter)* You are the creator of the movie.

Man:
That just can't be.

The Monitor:
It is true. You can think about it if you'd like. *(Laughter)* Do you have any more questions or is the dream over?

Man:
I would like to know if you have walked through a wall.

The Monitor:
No, I usually give examples of things in my own experience, but I did not want to give you something that you could not take in.

Man:
Such as?

The Monitor:
You want to see?

Man:
Yes.

....

An image appears. The men see a holographic image of a woman, the same elder woman, in meditation. She is just sitting and looking ordinary. Suddenly, ordinary and extraordinary converge. The woman is simultaneously filled with the cosmos, nebulas, stars, moons, and suns. Music never heard touches hearing. And still the woman sits.

....

Man:
Do you expect us to believe that woman experienced cosmic consciousness and was aware beyond teachers, teachings, religions, and traditions?

The Monitor:
No, I expect nothing of you. It is up to you to open your heart and mind. It is up to you to desire beyond a crying birth, a couple beers, some good screws, and a miserable or even honorable death. It is up to you to cry out, "Is there something more? Is there meaning, purpose anywhere? Do I just work hard or not and retire and get sick?"

Man:
Who has time to ask those questions?

The Monitor:
Who does not have time? Time is your making. A belief in the mind.

Man:
Do you believe that?

The Monitor:
No, I don't. I know it. The distinction is great. It will serve you well, in time, to know it. *(Laughter)* Now I have a question for you. Why have you come into my dream?

Man:
We began to notice a change in women around us. Then we began to observe them. We even observed that some men are supporting these women in their strange ways. These women even talk about such things as the uprising feminine. You are one of them, only more extreme. Talking about things like cosmic consciousness.

The Monitor:
That does not tell me why you have come to me. You really want to know if this shift in women is true. I tell you this. You must find this knowing in yourSelf. You must know the Unknown to find the Known. Your orientation around the nouns —i.e., person, place, and things—does not help you. All the attention on the external world can cause you to be lost in the world of objects. That also includes thoughts. They are things. You can be lost in thought. It can put you in a trance. Actually mesmerize you. Stay instead open to feeling. Feel the inner Presence. I don't want to confuse you, but this inner Presence, your very own Self, is everywhere Present. Feeling this opens a seeming human mind to the Divine Mind that it is.

Man:
Give us a glimpse that is more believable.

The Monitor:
This is a simple example: I am an artist. When I paint, I paint, knowing it is for someone. Many times while painting, I have received phone calls of people telling me that they needed to, were prompted to call me in that moment. They want to know what I am doing at

that moment of now. I say I am painting and I tell them of the essence of the painting. They are amazed, saying that is what is happening in their life and that they must have the painting. So without seeing it and even before I am finished with it, they buy the painting. This simple example illustrates our Oneness. You call it a coincidence. I call it a co-incidents. Yes!

Man:
We are curious.

The Monitor:
Does that mean you would like another example?

Man:
Yes.

The Monitor:
You know when you told me of noticing women acting different and then observing them even closer? And then some of the men are even supporting them?

Man:
Yes.

The Monitor:
Well that is three of the four steps man goes though in making the shift in the new relationships with women.

Man:
What is the fourth?

The Monitor:
Standing beside them. Working with them, enjoying life

with them in equal partnership. Creating the new Earth, the new culture together. In Balance.

Man:
How did you know of these four phases of men?

The Monitor:
It was revealed in meditation in the 80s.

Man:
You mean to say we are experiencing now what you were shown years ago?

The Monitor:
I am saying that.

Man:
It is a little scary to hear things like that. People like that have been called witches.

The Monitor:
What, you want secrets? Or do you want transparent Mind? You might want to see how secrets serve you here or not? We are on the brink of blowing up the world because of secrets.

Man:
I am beginning to have some insight about what is possible.

The Monitor:
Shanti, why are you in this dream? You have been quiet all along.

Shanti:
I represent the emerging man of the new Earth. I want to

serve in any way I can. Mostly I play my guitar and sing of love.

The Monitor:
And why is your friend Joy in the dream? She keeps coming and going.

Shanti:
Joy has no desires besides joy. She smiles and hugs and wanders on.

Man:
What kind of a life is that?

Shanti:
Joy is contagious. The world needs joy. She desires to reveal the value of joy in the barren lives.

Man:
We have jumped all over the place. We were talking about why you are monitoring the Earth. Is it just parts of the Earth you monitor or the entire Earth, or does the question even matter?

The Monitor:
Yes, it matters. Those who monitor scan the entire Earth. There is no "part" of the Earth. The Earth is a whole. It is One. It is one single living organism. To narrow it down to a part would be to ignore the fact. The interrelatedness and interconnectedness is important.

Man:
You presume there is a unity.

The Monitor:
I presume nothing. I have experienced Unity.

Man:
What grand assumptions you have.

The Monitor:
You may dismiss the experience of anyone with such words. It will not change the experience. You may debate, argue, and chide. The experience stays the same.

I have an idea. You may consider this: Spend more time with what you describe as these strange women. Stay open. Stay receptive. See if they are more joyful than you. More fun. See if you laugh more. *(Laughter)* And men like Shanti. Hang out with them.

Man:
Is our talk coming to a close?

The Monitor:
I am going to meditate and get some sleep. It has been a long day to experience dream and dreamer as One. I did ask for it. I have loved our time together. I would love even to continue, if you would like to return. Your questions actually serve me.

Man:
Why do they serve you?

The Monitor:
When you ask me questions, I get clarity on my own life. You gift me with the ability to see with growing clarity.

Maybe my glasses will come off sooner than I thought. Vision is important.

Man:
We would like to return.

....

The next day arrives.

....

The Monitor:
I was thinking of you early this morning and just wondering if you had heard of Atlantis and Lemuria?

Man:
Vaguely. Are you going to tell us that you believe the fantasies about those civilizations are real?

The Monitor:
No, that is not what I am going to say. Here is what I am going to ask you to consider.

Two things. One is that if you will open your heart and unclench your mind, which is like a fist ready to strike anything, you will discover that truth will reveal itself to you. Quite effortlessly.

Man:
Give a current example.

The Monitor:
If you wish to know about an animal, follow it around, live with it, and even breathe with it. Watch it gift you

with its secrets. Rather in the Dr. Jane Goodall tradition. It amounts to nothing but murder and unceasing suffering to trap it, take it to a lab, kill it, dissect it, analyze it, and write volumes of texts about its guts and brains and call it a university course. It serves no one. It seems to serve those receiving large cash amounts in the name of science, called research and development. We have developed cruelty unprecedented as we have harmed these beings.

What we need to include in R and D is the study of what is known as the human species. What we need to do is study Consciousness. What we need to take seriously is "Man, Know Thyself."

Man:
What is the second thing you want us the know about Atlantis and Lemuria?

The Monitor:
If you read the book *Edgar Cayce's Atlantis and Lemuria*, you will unmistakingly see that this moment in present time is a perfect example of history repeating itself. It is a crossroads, exactly as that time was. The heart and mind of the human species were not working together. Atlantis lived in the mind and for that reason came to have selfish purposes for the good of a selfish few. Lemuria was in the heart and did all the good for the whole. Do you begin to see where I am going? Atlantis was in the misuse of technology created to serve a few. The inviolate universal Law of Balance was being broken then. It is being broken now.

Man:
Say more.

The Monitor:
Open your eyes and see the special interests of corporations and governments, even. Open your eyes and see the abuse of women. For God's sake, the women and children are still considered the booty of men's wars and raped and tortured, often with permanent impairment. Even now. Put yourselves in their lives and bodies if you can. Many of them don't have shoes for you to step in. The Dalai Lama would say have compassion. I say, see yourself as their life. More than compassion will arise. The courage to change will arise. The "lost protector" of the women and children will arise. Where the hell have you been? In the shifting sands of instability, you have tried to get ahead and to hoard a retirement. Get ahead! Think about that. Get ahead of who? Is life a race? Are we here to show off? Is it all one big competition?

Man:
Are you ridiculing men?

The Monitor:
Your question is just one more way that you create an excuse to continue in the battle of heart and mind. Atlantis and Lemuria continue on. Your question has only been a poorly devised crutch that you will need to outgrow if change is to come.

Man:
Aren't there women that are in the battle as well? And who are asleep?

The Monitor:
Of course. Many of them. The power of the heart is great. However, giving too much is as great an imbalance as taking too much. Women must learn the lesson of not giving too much. These are the women you have noticed. The ones you call strange women. The pain of that imbalance is now so great that they must get out of the condition. It is as confining as any cage in a zoo or lab or industrial stockyard that removes the freedom to be. Do you think for a moment that you are seeing a true lion in a zoo? You are seeing the pacing and dullness of a confined being, unfree to live its life in its natural habitat. Some animals in zoos go insane because of the caging. Perhaps the women who have gone seemingly insane and are institutionalized were also reacting to their cage.

Man:
Are you referring to the entirety of the patriarchy as a cage?

The Monitor:
I am. It is so obvious. To pretend otherwise is the real insanity here. I heard that psychologists call it gaslighting. The popular name is crazymaking. It means to say one thing and then pretend you said or did something else.

Man:
You are getting amusing now.

The Monitor:
I am only describing what has been happening for eons to the women. To cry "accuser" is only to run away pretending a little longer. Why would you want to let go

of control? Without it, you fear you will not get what you want. You lack trust. And there has been little inclination to gain it. Legions of women are leading the way. They are finding out where Trust comes from. What is the origin of Trust? How does one live in Trust?

Man:
Are you going to share how to get Trust?

The Monitor:
If I say too much, you will say I am starting a new religion. Frankly, I feel all religions will eventually decompose, like the day's compost, perhaps using the beautiful buildings to truly teach how to live life in Trust. And get grand results in life! At this point, the name of the religious structure will be irrelevant. Who cares the name of the ladder that delivered the person to that which is the Wordless and the Nameless One?

The Love that is entering the world cannot be described with human words. And, hey, it does not mean sitting on your knees in a pew seven days a week. The Holy Rollers might be closer to the Truth. At least there is a celebration. Dancing and Singing.

Man:
So are you monitoring the genders?

The Monitor:
The awakening is not a gender issue. In fact, it is the place inside your heart wherein you experience the marriage of your own yin and yang. Without a minister. Without a medium of any kind. Without an audience or

congregation. Your own masculine and feminine. They do wed and know. Androgyny…it is.

Man:
O my God, are you saying men and women won't pair up anymore?

The Monitor:
Not at all. The pairing will be authentic and it will be equal. There will be balance. It is an exciting time. These are the new movies. Epic even. Men have been scared to death for the power of the Infinite through the feminine to take form. That time is over. The new Partners in Purpose are emerging. When you begin to be aware of this, you will notice them everywhere.

Man:
Can we buy a book on the subject?

The Monitor:
These partners are writing and their stories are good. However, they are their stories. There are not manuals to be memorized. If there are, be leary of them. The partners are listening within. They are wayshowers and pioneers. They are not to be copied. They are to reveal it is possible. All the way around, it is an inner joy. It must emerge out of a joined heart and mind. The self and the Self, one and the same. You may also look at visionary art about these sacred partners in such books as *The Sacred Two*. Allow yourself to be inspired for this in your own life.

Man:
This looks like tremendous work and inner struggle.

The Monitor:
That is merely the appearance. It is not a surrender or a release of all that you have in the world. It is taking all attention away from the external world that you believe will make you happy. Surrender is not a workshop or a ritual. Surrender is putting your attention on the internal Consciousness that is Spirit. In that, all can come to you.

Man:
Reads like a fairy tale.

The Monitor:
The fairies might tell you it is a fairy tale and if you listen, they, too, will instruct and guide you in the in-between world.

Man:
Now, to boot, you are telling us to believe in fairies and even to listen to them. Even saying they have wisdom to share. A relevant voice.

The Monitor:
I am not telling you that. I am saying this: Consider asking to know the truth. You might consider not dismissing things as fantasy and fiction just because you have believed only what you were taught, heard, or read in a narrow world. Know truth for yourSelf. Stay open to truth. That way, beliefs, for or against, can dissolve back into the substance of creation. There are way too many beliefs floating through this lightwave, thought wave universe. They are like thieves. They steal the Real Life. And the Real Life becomes invisible to our eyes, covered by our beliefs.

Man:
Have you seen a fairy?

The Monitor:
I have only experienced one fairy while I sat solitary in the woods a few years back. I could not see her, but I could feel her Presence.

Man:
How do you know, really know, it was a fairy?

The Monitor:
How do you know, really know, that you feel you must visit a person? For no reason. You just know it. Growing the intuition opens a world of seeming thrill and mystery. Daily you walk into the Great Unknown, the Great Mystery. We are rewriting Don Quixote… together.

Man:
You make the shift, the change, sound fun at times.

The Monitor:
Imagine this! When you get excited about being with a woman you are attracted to, you are feeling and sensing her Mystery. You sometimes believe that the only way to own or access that Mystery is through copulation. With woman out of the cage you will behold the Mystery in motion, in dance and song. It is bursting forth around the planet. This kundalini in woman is aroused. The fire of the new Earth is setting the world aglow with an Illumination unprecedented. The dark ages, even now, just embers of the past.

Man:

It seems that you are suggesting that if we in any way hang on to old patterns, old modes of being and thinking, that we will heap great pain upon our lives.

The Monitor:

You must live life as you want. The Earth, however, is in the act of the Dance of Oneness. The rebalancing going on is affecting all. To resist is to create disaster in one's own life. Imbalance carries the seeds of its own destruction.

Man:

Put that way, it seems that we don't have a choice.

The Monitor:

You may choose the seeming separation until it consumes you or you may choose yourSelf. Why would anyone entertain choosing other than their Self? That would be utterly ridiculous. When I started realizing that, in my own life, I began to shift. Choosing the antithesis of the Self is the same as suicide. Sorry to be so graphic. Think about it. Draw your own conclusions. They will probably be the hysterical rewrite of all of history. His Story, the patriarchy, masculine domination. We are now adding Her Story to find out the True Story.

Man:

You have a way of making it sound intriguing.

The Monitor:

Enter front stage! The new Epic Story of Balance. What do you have to bring to the story?

Man:
I don't know.

The Monitor:
Don't you want to know? Do you want to sit on the sidelines of the sports arena, the coliseum of Rome, yet again? Do you not get bored as a bystander? The only thing that then sounds exciting is creating another war. Excitement, thrill, action, killing! You like that one as a spectator sport, as well. The veterans come home with another perspective. If they come home at all. Listen to their stories of battles to plunder and take from one another. Tales of woe. Just like taking candy from a child in kindergarten. The roots for the act of taking have been deep for eons. These are the only weeds we need remove, not the beautiful herbs trying to show up in the garden.

Man:
You make it sound easy, like we could become weed pickers for a career. How unreal is that?

The Monitor:
I can see it now: www.mentalweedremoval.com. Coaches available to find the mental weeds that cover your waiting ecstasy of life. Enter here: non-duality.

Man:
O my God. You did mean it.

The Monitor:
(*Laughter*) I did. Use your imagination. Where there is demand, supply comes. It comes when called, right out of the Substance of Creation. Well, the demand is growing.

The supply needs to be ready. The new culture is sprouting and leafing even now. Flowering is already upon us!

Man:
Well, it would create new jobs, new careers.

The Monitor:
There you go again, always thinking of money. As if economics was the Purpose of Life. The marketplace of life is very simple. It is love in action.

Man:
How hilarious! You haven't been to market much.

The Monitor:
Love in action is the living of the Law of Balance. It is the real and equal giving and regiving from the heart. That is the action in all of Nature. Hinduism has a goddess by the name of Saraswati. She is the goddess of reciprocity. I can just see Saraswati taking over Wall Street or teaching in the universities. I ask you, "What does that look like?" It is a new order and no one is in control. A true Self-governing has emerged. Smiles form everywhere.

Man:
You seem to imply that there has been great irresponsible behavior in the business world.

The Monitor:
No, it is not an implication. It is a statement of fact. Business is failing and flailing when it is not fair. Fair Trade in the marketplace has already birthed to a small degree. What does that mean? It clearly means to clear the

stage for the dance of Saraswati. Her hips are swinging now.

....

Image of a grand dancer dressed as Saraswati with music of that time dancing across the stage in front of the two men. She swings her hips in the joy!

....

Man:
Are you trying to make fairness in business seductive so that change can come?

The Monitor:
Whatever works. I really do not care how "the come" comes, but surely you yourselves know that the wiles of Beauty could lead the way. Dogs always sniff when the female is in heat. And the females of the world are in heat. They are ready to birth a whole new world. In fact, many, many men have already made the change, as well. They are androgynous and they too are birthing the new culture.

Man:
Now you have men birthing. I wondered if we should listen to you in the first place. You are one of the strange ones.

The Monitor:
These men are all around you. Rub the sleep from your eyes. I am going for a walk. You are welcome to return, unless this dream is complete.

Man:

A couple of questions before you leave. Do you like being a monitor? It seems rather judgmental at this point.

The Monitor:

Learn the difference between judging and a simple statement about the law of balance being violated. Another way of saying it is that the emperor has no clothes. As far as liking to be a monitor, let me put it this way: Presence functions as a monitor through me. It is that simple. There are entire organizations that are monitoring the care of the planet.

Man:

Name one.

The Monitor:

www.EarthWatch.org It is a role played by Spirit. It's even a little like a mother watching that her child does not burn its hand in the fire.

Man:

Are you actually comparing yourself to the Mother of the World? We have heard some of the other strange women talk of the Earth mother.

The Monitor:

It is not a comparison. When women who are mothers of the home wake up, they open also to Mother of the World. It is not an identity. It is a function. And it is not a religion, nor is it some exclusive role, saved for a few. In fact, it is a lot of work.

Man:
So now you think you are a Mother of the World?

The Monitor:
I detect sneer, sarcasm, and disbelief. That is your shield blinding your vision. The world has long had Fathers of the World. Six thousand years. Alone they create chaos, war, and endless pain and destruction. Still are. History and a simple newspaper are the proof.

Without the balance of love, care, protection, nourishing, men seem to blow up the world. Yes, the world needs a mother. For Balance. And now. In fact, all women are invited. Mothers of the World positions are now being offered by the Cosmos. The pay is good. Saved will be the human species. And an illumined species, already happening, will continue to be evident.

Man:
You are optimistic.

The Monitor:
You are asleep. And you cannot see what is. What already is!

Man:
We want to know how you found optimism!

The Monitor:
Leave your mind, your thinking.

Man:
Go out of our minds?

The Monitor:
That is it! Some people call it meditation. If that puts you off, call it what you want. Find the Silence, the peace that lives ever within you and more accurately, lives AS you, as you allow.

Man:
That is scary again. We have worked a lifetime to be in control and to create, and you are asking us to relinquish control.

The Monitor:
In this Place of Silence within is the Spiritual Universe. Find that Place. Return and share it with all of us. It is called in spiritual texts the pearl of great price. Then… optimism…it is yours.

Man:
You are bordering on sounding preachy.

The Monitor:
(Laughter) It only sounds like that because you don't want to know. You are not yet yin or receptive enough. I think the dream is complete. Good day. Or should I say, bad day, since you are not optimistic.

Man:
Are you getting sarcastic?

The Monitor:
No, I am speaking to you from where you are. I like to call it the entry point of conversation.

Man:
You mean that you speak differently to us than to others.

The Monitor:
Yes, that is what I mean.

Man:
Why did you choose to be interviewed by two men from the sleeping collective archetype?

The Monitor:
It seemed to seep in through the dream state when I was not conscious. Remember, I could glide from the zone between dream and waking until they seemed to be one. I was not even sure who was asking, me or you. And is there any difference?

Man:
Now you are getting very esoteric or New Age!

The Monitor:
Then talk to the Mayans. A favored greeting is In Lak'ech. It means "I Am another yourSelf." Isn't that beautiful? A good line to ponder. Especially before one goes to war.

Man:
So why the interviewing?

The Monitor:
I have tried to speak to many on these subjects. I was met with disbelief too often. This way I can dream up the question for the Answer I have found. I have an insight and now I can formulate it as a question. Is it fact or fiction? It is for you to decide.

Man:

What a setup! What an ultimate manipulation. Very woman like.

The Monitor:

It seems so, but the insights drop in from a Place that does not even care about the world of duality. It is impervious to evil. It is ever fully immune.

Man:

Is this part of what you want us to believe that you saw in Cosmic Consciousness?

The Monitor:

I told you I did not care what you believe. I am just dancing upon the Earth, painting, writing poetry with seeds of invitation. There is a big party. A celebration of sorts. No one will be left behind unless they choose.

Man:

For a while this was sounding fun; now it is sounding serious, even ominous, like a gathering storm.

The Monitor:

As you please.

Man:

You are not even going to bribe us or prod us on?

The Monitor:

What good would that do? Woman has played that game for eons. And hideous war or the brink of war never ceases in this country or that. It is like a festering sore coming out of one part of the body or another. We add a chemical and think we are done, not wanting to know it is often systemic. What is happening has been systemic. Remember, we are one living organism.

Man:
Anything more about choosing, unconsciously or not, two men for this interview we are all in?

The Monitor:
I love this. *(Laughter)* I have interviewers and they are also the audience. And I choose the questions for you based on my insights.

Man:
So is this some sort of new genre? It is not fiction, nor is it non-fiction. It is not even in novel form or screen play form. Just endless questions and answers. That joyful Place in the Silence might have more imagination than that. Comedy even.

The Monitor:
I am enjoying the form. Immensely.

Man:
You just won't let up.

Other man:
Isn't the title, *The Monitor and Laughter of the Gods,* a little flat?

The Monitor:
I did consider naming it *The Ultimate Ravage of the Gods* or *Revenge of the Gods,* knowing I would get a larger audience. *(Laughter)* The world of duality loves violence

and endless terror. I guess I could change the title later if this does not attract enough folks. But the audience might walk out when they see they have been duped, with no blood and agony. Either way, that won't work. I will stay open to a more attractive title. Sex always works. I could use *Saraswati Comes Swingin' Her Hips*. *(Laughter)*

Man:
A couple more questions.

Other man:
Don't you think the audience will be put off with the constant reference to words like seduction, the come, sex, copulation since you are doing your big Purity Revolution?

The Monitor:
It is possible, but if they open their eyes wider, from the exhausted droop of duality woes, they will see that, wow, we live in an electrically sexed universe of pure science. All, I mean all, of the universe is participating. I assure you that it is not hidden behind closed black doors of forbidden sex. It might be happening behind closed eyes, but not doors. It is naked. And all of Nature, hey, not just man, woman, and the animals, are attracting each other. How do we think we got water? H_2O. Sex again! One grand universal sexual intercourse, if we care to see. Orgasm. Again and again. It is intimate. It is precious.

It is out in the open for all to see, feel, experience. It is alchemy of the highest sort. It is pure. It was never dirty. Contraction and expansion, evaporate and precipitate, in and out, nail and nail hole, up and down. Opposites but no opposition. Opposites in the Dance of the One. The universe is celebrating the marriage of yin and yang, masculine and feminine, in every moment. Hot and cold looking for balance in warm. What a show! And we are missing the show. We have mistaken the opposite in the dance of the one, as opposition, battle, and ceaseless war in the home, nations, and world home. If we are not exhausted by now, we should at least be bored out of our minds.

Six thousand years. Same old epic battle of good and evil as a guise for life, promulgated in movies, books, plays, scriptures, and governments, and on. And we eat it up along with popcorn and soda pop. The battles continue and we are entertained.

Man:
We thought you would never end taking the stage there.

The Monitor:
If you will but notice, there is a new stage. It is creating from Vision. From Spirit. Choose now which stage.

Man:
That sounded like a threat. Choose now.

The Monitor:
There is only now. Whenever, it will still be now. It is not a threat. It is an invitation. Before our interview, you did not even know there was another stage already borne and even being lived upon.

Man:
This is our last question.

Other man:
We have read of prophecy and civilizations through the ages forecasting Armageddon and doom and endless gloom. You know. The end of the world. What do you think of that?

The Monitor:
I read recently in an article by a Bible student that over one-third of the Bible is prophecy. Whether it is that high or not, I don't know, but certainly people for 2000+ years have been projecting and outpicturing the worst for the world. One might ask what the quantum physicists would say here. Any connection?

I am back now to ask you a question. What was the intent here? Certainly deep fears have been conditioned and bred.

Man:
What do you think of the actual act of prophecy?

The Monitor:
You don't want me to talk about my experience in Cosmic Consciousness, but I can answer the question better from the direct revelation. There is only ever Consciousness and it is in harmony. Therein lies the answer. It is so simple. People themselves make it complex when it is not.

Prophecies made by true seers and seeresses are valuable in the world. They point out areas where we are harming, not caring. They point out that inexorable principles of the universe have been broken with acts of imbalance. In that, the prophecies are great portents of truth. They are great messengers. They are signals. They are warnings. They are the Voice of Change. If the warning is heeded, the prophecy need not come to pass. All prophesies are subject to change. That change is upon us. We are that change. So why focus on and fear and feed the prophecy? Instead, focus on what is yours to do in the creation of a new culture and Earth.

Man:
How can we do that if we do not know what form that is? Is there someone to go to?

The Monitor:
Yes. That someone is you.

Man:
Aren't you afraid you will be branded as irreverent?

The Monitor:
The ways and wars of the ages have been irreverent.

Man:
Could you leave us with a message that motivates?

The Monitor:
There is a great distinction between motivation and inspiration. One is mental and one is from your very Self.

Man:
It is as if more than one world is existing side by side simultaneously.

The Monitor:
That is so.

Man:
There are many unanswered questions.

The Monitor:
Only so long as they are ignored.

Man:
You are fierce.

The Monitor:
It only seems so.

Man:
Who are we? Why did we come to visit in your dream?

The Monitor:
Does it matter?

Man:
Then what matters?

The Monitor:
This is what I hoped you would ask!

What matters is this:
What is your part?
What is your dream?
What Action is borne in your heart?

....

Laughter of the Gods…with recording going into echo getting fainter and fainter.

Then…

the chorus creates a procession dancing and singing across the stage. They stand as Saraswati, the goddess of reciprocity, dances across the stage to Her music.

© 2008, 2013 Mary Saint-Marie

All Rights reserved. No part of this dramatization may be reproduced in any form or by any electronic or mechanical means, including information storage and retrieval systems, without permission in writing from the author.

The Monitor as a Messenger of Balance

The Monitor's role in the play is as a messenger of the sacred balance. Nature's ever-present universal law of balance. She is a lucid observer of the events in the world. A witness. A monitor.

Though caring, The Monitor has a detached demeanor. She is not involved in the choices that humanity makes. She has no opinion where humanity goes. She sees and she reports. And she offers understanding.

With that understanding, humanity may understand The Mystical as the Practical, the "as above, so below" in all of our lives. Humanity may understand and finally realize that by connecting with the higher dimensions, life on this planet will change. Harmony may come. And love that has no conditions. Joy shall come on stage! And Shanti, the peace.

The Monitor represents the no-mind, often called the right brain of humanity. She is the pure Consciousness. Transparent Mind. A human mind that is open to the One Mind.

The Monitor represents a powerful, often ignored, archetypal force of the divine feminine principle that exists in woman and in man. She is not representing a gender, but a principle, a set of values that reveals equality, nobility, caring, receptivity, and great Intelligence. It is the ancient wisdom that resides, even now, within our hearts. And a new humanity and a new culture does emerge.

The sights of The Monitor have been set beyond the dreary and dramatized norm, yet she still can enjoy the humor of it all without being flippant or judgmental. Laughter fills her life. She lives beyond the stereotypes of woman and of man on the Earth, yet she is still here on the Earth as a messenger. She is depicted and portrayed as a messenger that would offer the departure from the clutches of the insanity of a belief in separation from the One.

In her field, a happiness fills the air.

The Two Men as World Catalysts

The two men in the play represent ones, men and women, who have lived out of balance and harmony with nature and life itself. They represent ones who have been living mainly from the masculine principle, the yang of creation. They represent ones who have been living in their human minds, cut off from a higher mind. Divine Mind. Devoid of guidance.

However, the play is, in part, a tribute to these men who have been drunk with mental oblivion. For now they are strong and awake enough to honor and respect the divine feminine nature of our beings, in themselves and in woman. They open, hesitantly at first, to the yin and yang balance that lives as all of nature.

These two men portray man and woman, that are awakening out of their outmoded and antiquated condescending attitudes and conditioned beliefs toward the universal feminine principle. They are awakening out of the linear, left brain world of seeming separation.

The role of the two men, though having few lines in the script, is very important in this global awakening upon us all. They are between the two worlds. The old paradigm and a new emerging Earth. They stand powerfully for the old paradigm waking up and yet they birth as messengers to those still stuck in a world of beliefs. They begin to see. They see that there is more to existence.

In the dream/awake experience, the men are still in the deep observing stage with what they call "this strange woman." There exists in them a genuine disbelief and curiosity. They are filled with questions. There is no disdain, nor is there mockery. No sharpness.

When the men observe "the strange women," they are attracted. They like what they see. It is new. It is life filled. They are even mesmerized, yet still they have some, "Huh, how could this be true?" registering. They are not unconscious mankind speaking. They reveal an awakening Consciousness.

The two men find themselves in a very subtle zone between the demeaning attitude of the old paradigm and the new. In the new way of balance, there is a recognition of their own feminine principle and of their own true nature in a universal sense.

These two men are truly a catalyst for the arising feminine values in humanity to birth a new culture.

These men have no need to misuse humor and tone as an attitude to degrade the values of the feminine principle.

They embody, at their own pace, the role of this beautifully awakening divine feminine principle on the planet in all beings. Thus it can be honored in all of nature.

Housed in the new Earth is balance.

The Essence of Saraswati

SHE…is the womb of creation…
the cradle of civilization…

SHE…is the birther supreme…
the mother of all…

SHE…is the nurturer and protector…
the fierce guardian of earth…

SHE…is the voice of love…
giving rise to the pure…

We are living in a time on the sacred planet Earth when the Timeless is finding its way into the lives of millions. This Timeless realm is represented in the play, *The Monitor and Laughter of the Gods,* as the Goddess Saraswati. Her essence of that Timeless realm may be felt and realized by ones everywhere.

The essence dance of Saraswati inspires a dance that lives within us all. And it is urgent.

Each of us may align with this presence of life itself and feel this essence arising and living as our very being and doing.

Saraswati has been portrayed in this play in the way that she was unveiled to me as essence on the inner planes when I received the play.

In the play, The Monitor is known as one who sees through the eyes of purity. And Saraswati, who has sometimes been called the Goddess of Purity and Transcendence, is the dancing messenger for purity. Without purity, the world does enter a destructive manner of expression.

One might remember that a similar message of the Hopi has been given; they speak of this time as the time of purification.

Saraswati enters the stage, in the play, to dance when the business and economic world is discussed as failing in its blatant lack of equal giving and regiving which is the universal law of balance. Saraswati enters on stage when she sees this inviolate law being broken in the marketplace. Saraswati dances upon the stage as invincible, as a carrier of the inner knowledge and wisdom of reciprocity in this universe of yin and yang in equal measure. Inexorable. And she does dance.

Traditionally, Saraswati, a Hindu Goddess, has been described in many ways. World Mother. Goddess of Beauty, Dance, Music, Wisdom, Knowledge, the Arts. Patron Saint of Musicians. She is associated with the veena and accompanied by peacock and swan. She reveals the wisdom of the Vedas. She has been called the mother of humanity.

Saraswati, whose name means "the essence of the self," does lead us home to the inner purity that is pure consciousness that manifests as a world of beauty.

The World of Shanti, Joy, and The Wise Woman

The world of Shanti, Joy, and The Wise Woman is the awake world. Here…love, joy, and wisdom emanate from everyone. Here…peace is a quality of the inner life…lived. It is not something to fight for, nor to sign endless ignored or broken treaties for. A deeper horizon has been seen, felt, and known.

Shanti, who carries the name that is the Sanskrit word for peace and bliss, lives on a frequency of a world beyond division, beyond false beliefs and beyond boundaries created in the ever-human mind devoid of love. He abides in the place in Consciousness where life is realized as music. So he plays. And he sings. And the Soul of humanity hears the call.

When Shanti sings, Joy dances. Joy is the sacred movement of Life as dance. She is as a bee, drunk on the elixir of the flowers. She is as a pied piper calling in more awakened ones. Ever does she dance. Ever does she dance The Formless life into form. Ever does she embody that which makes us smile.

And the Wise Woman. O this woman does see with eyes of fire. She consumes ignorance. She pierces lies. She arrives with searing Presence. And she wanders on. She uses no words, yet she comes as the voice of the Awakening. And she is felt as an unyielding call to higher realms and dimensions. She represents the ever-expanding Consciousness that is humanity and life itself.

In *The Monitor and Laughter of the Gods,* we are called to dwell in higher dimensions. We are called to move from human thinking and reasoning to direct knowing. We are called to the emptiness that is the fullness.

It is here that symbolism departs and we see that we are those seeming characters in the play. The sacred theatre does live within us all. We are those glimpses, those experiences, those realizations.

The world of Shanti, Joy, and The Wise Woman is the ancient remembering of a world beyond limits.

It is the garden world we erroneously seek outside ourselves in fiction, movies, and never-ending drama.

It is the world that awaits our seeing…

It is a world where self is known as Self. One. And Self-governing upon this land is that which is birthing, even now, the new Earth.

We are the very ones that do unveil the Mystery.

The World Home

The Monitor and Laughter of the Gods is relevant to the present world drama and serves as an avenue of illumination. It serves as a bringer of change.

A simple study and aerial view of history reveals that there has been primarily a dominator culture for five to six thousand years. A time when the masculine principle has dominated the feminine principle and values of caring, giving, loving, beauty on this planet. Great inequalities have occurred in the home and in the world home. The yang and yin out of balance has yielded great suppression, oppression, repression, depression and endless outer impressions and pressures in individuals and societies. It has yielded suffering. What is desired is expression from the withinness, the Oneness. From the inner knowing and awareness to the outer manifestation. And change…it comes.

The One as Many…in the One Dance upon Life's stage.

Sacred Theatre as life itself.

The Monitor is simply a reminder to come out from under the lie of that imbalance of the last 6000 years.

The Monitor is a reminder that initiates the arising of the divine feminine values in all of humanity to work in harmony with the masculine principle.

The Monitor is a reminder of the universal law of balance in all of nature, that the people may together create an unprecedented culture…a gathering of light. Beauty!

The Monitor is a reminder that we need a Mother of the World Home, as well as a Father of the World Home. It is clear that the past imbalance did not birth joy, abundance, wholeness, love, equality, or justice.

And now…together we can allow the Universal Balance that Already Is…and birthed…together…is the new and numinous culture…

Soul Responses to the Play

Many people spoke to me directly after the play, sharing their insights and feelings about the play. I distinctly remember one magnificent elder who came up to me and said, "Honey, you said it all."

Others stopped me on the street and in the market for days and weeks after the showing of *The Monitor and Laughter of the Gods,* telling me of their inner experience as part of the audience. Others called and emailed me.

I decided to include a few of the unsolicited responses, as I fully realized during the performances that the audience was Conscious, Awake, open, supportive, and responding. The audience was an integral part of the communication and the experience. Truly a co-creation.

I am grateful to all of you.

These responses may serve to "speak" to those who have not witnessed the stage version of the play and see it through the soul of some of the audience and an actor.

"I wanted to write and let you know how wonderful I thought The Monitor and Laughter of the Gods was. I LOVED the play. I thought that it was perfection, from the woman who played the lead, to the way the play was structured with the question/answer format, to the division of intent and content from Act 1 to Act 11.

There are so many levels, layers, and messages to be absorbed. I found myself wishing that I was able to watch a rehearsal where I would have a note pad to take down all of the insights that occurred for me. I was struck by the fact that the audience was filled with so many of your loving friends from Mt. Shasta, who are like-minded, but had a strong sense that the play was done in a way that is so palatable for a wider audience of people, who might just be starting to awaken.

My husband is early in the journey and he also thought it was fantastic. He mentioned that in another format some of the subject matter might be hard for some men to take in, but that in the way that it was done in The Monitor, it flowed so easily and was so gently done that it was expansive and opening.

The woman who played the lead did such a marvelous job of channeling you, without that being the intent. The result of her performance was the transference of beauty and pure essence of consciousness, in such a glorious way that the room, the air and the energy was filled with light. It was beautiful to watch and to experience.

So...Thank you for moving forward with what you were given to bring forth in the form of a play and making it available to all of us. I am so happy that we were able to be in Ashland for the opening."

~ Denise Gilbert, visionary photographer

"Thank you! It was completely my pleasure to be there to see so much of Mary and Truth out in front of everybody "on stage." Well, it was great. Very nice to see the dream from the dream weekend appear on stage like we were a part of it during the early planting and then the harvest.

I loved the Joy dancing—felt very much like home. I also got to see in a lot of ways how fierce doesn't equal harsh. Fierce is the front line of standing in Truth and stating or calling out the boundary—I really like that. I did not really get it until the play—because I really do live in a soft gentle world, I have not had exposure to a lot of events that other women have experienced—and so having it stated so clearly showed me it is still ok to be "fierce" about the boundaries and, well, what better way for us to help others learn where the lines are located? The lines of choice—and I felt the audience was so wide awake— sitting with a group that large and awake—well, magic happens.

Also Saraswati's dance was not like any type of "belly dance" we have seen before—it was feminine and gentle, like moving energy around in that, with her body, and yet without tones of sex. Her smile was beatific and knowing—like everything she touches with her dance and scarf and toes, and all were really seeing the feminine spirit in 3D dance.

And for Kate—well I will just say she had the same Mary twinkle, and I wonder how you will teach that?

And oh my—there is no doubt in my mind you have held the torch and placed light on this play from start to finish to keep it as whole and complete as it was when you did the writing."

~ Laura Hamill, visionary artist and teacher of Painting Wild

"Thank you so much for allowing us to receive the truth of your experience. It was profound, and the leading lady held her own as your voice, with the supporting actors weaving their reflective lens right alongside of her; each in his own unique way. The piece, itself, allowed us to contemplate our own inner landscapes, and how we can choose to set boundaries that honor us as we each carve the experience of our own individual canvas—a Creative Journey of Self—simultaneously BEcoming the observer and the receiver."

~ Dorothea Joyce, mystic singer, songwriter, performer, author

"*What a Great Play you Birthed!*

I can't begin to tell you in words what this Special Play meant to me, in the moment and in my personal life!!!! It has added to and opened up my Heart anew for the Calling of the One!!!"

~ Dennis Nicomede, visionary poet and actor who was in the play

About the Artist/Writer

After leaving high school and college English teaching, writing curriculum and working as an assistant coordinator and liaison in Public Educational TV, Mary began her more bohemian and creative life as a mystic artist and later as a mystic writer, as a result of a near death experience in a car collision that totaled both cars. Mary saw her life in full… past, present, and future at the moment of impact, when she said, "God, I am yours." Mary entered the soul realm of pure joy. After that, Mary could see the emanations of the field of light, commonly called an aura, around all living things. She had deeply opened to the light of love that we all already are. And her life changed. Mary began to pioneer visionary art shows in Oregon in 1972, creating her first three art exhibits during a journey across the Middle East, India, and into Kashmir.

After much free spirit traveling around the globe and nation, Mary called inwardly for guidance in finding a perfect place to raise her daughter and to deepen her inner connection with this Light. More external desires began to fall away.

Shortly after, in 1974, Mary was led by a dream to the mountains of Northern California. She has lived close to nature since that time, as it was her childhood teacher and solace. It was there that she was embraced by grace.

Mary Saint-Marie's Art-of-the-Soul has been viewed at over 150 exhibits, in galleries, expositions, conferences, wholistic faires, and workshops across the country. It has been exhibited in workshops in Europe and the Yucatan. Mary's art is in private art collections around the world. The visionary art has been featured in numerous TV interviews and in books, magazines, and cards.

The Monitor and Laughter of the Gods is the eighth published book by Mary. In addition, Mary has two CDs that may be viewed on her website. *Journey of Consciousness* is a guided journey to experience the One Self. It is a Soul or Christed Initiation that allows one to experience one's Self as the Light of Consciousness, the I Am Awareness. The other CD is *Soul Sounds of World Birth*; it is soul sounding as a portal into the Light of Presence. In both CDs, Mary's voice is a catalyst.

Mary performed for seven years in multi-media sacred enactments called *She…it is…who Remembers,* taken from her book *Galactic Shamanism*. The enactments include her art, narration, soul sounding, dancing, and the sounds of guest musicians and the gifts of light technicians.

Then came *The Monitor and Laughter of the Gods,* a story of the urgently needed balance of the masculine and feminine principles. It is sacred theatre providing Awareness of our Oneness.

The Monitor and Laughter of the Gods is the first original play that Mary Saint-Marie has written. It is not conventional in format and was written inside of a weekend retreat without any plans to write. It just flowed forth as stream of consciousness.

Paintings, Art Exhibits, Soul Sessions, The Holy Sight Workshops, Books, and CDs

Mary Saint-Marie is a spiritual educator working with people who have come to her from around the world and nation.

....

Art of the Soul:
Ancient Beauty Studio by appointment
Original paintings and giclee fine art reproductions available
Bronze sculpture available
Conferences, symposiums, exhibitions

Soul Sessions: For individuals, by phone or in person, or will travel to another town/city if there is a coordinator

Soul Remembering Retreats: For individuals, in person, and lasting 1/2 day

The Holy Sight Workshop: Experiential work for groups

Books: May be ordered through Amazon.com

The Holy Sight
The Animating Presence
Messages from the Silence
Nectar of Woman
The Sacred Two
The Star-Stone Ones
Galactic Shamanism

CDs: May be ordered through the artist

Journey of Consciousness
Soul Sounds of World Birth

Sounds and Signings of the Soul: Individual initiations into sacred soul sounds and sacred soul movements/dance, that one is in one's soul expression of Life

Journey through the Kingdoms and Journey through the Elements: Individual initiations into feeling, seeing and/or being aware of one's Oneness with Kingdoms and the Elements, that one is in the I Am Awareness in nature

The Sacred Two: Initiation into the ancient yin-yang circle to be aware of the World Birth of Balance, the SHE and HE of Creation, to be aware of the Law of Love…the One come as the Partners in Purpose

SHE…it is…who Remembers: A Sacred Enactment of Ancient Remembering: Multi-media sacred theatre with art, dance, sacred sound, narration, music and shadow effects, from the book *Galactic Shamanism* by Mary Saint-Marie

Recordings: Inquire about purchase of recordings

SHE…it is…who Remembers: A poetic odyssey and narration of a portion of *Galactic Shamanism*

Return to Oneness: Recording of a poetic odyssey into the soul of the animal realm and their rights upon this earth

Poetic Odyssey Readings: Request information

EarthCare Global TV: Request information on the vision of a profound unification of global earth care

www.MarySaintMarie.com

www.EarthCareGlobalTV.com

Additional Plays or a Documentary

Please be in touch with the playwright, Mary Saint-Marie, if you are inspired to use this play/sacred enactment in your local theatre.

Also, please inquire about turning the play/sacred theatre into a documentary/drama that would travel to film festivals around the world, as another way to awaken the people to what they really are. Already are. Pure Consciousness. I Am Awareness.

Notes

Notes

Notes

Notes

Notes

www.ingramcontent.com/pod-product-compliance
Lightning Source LLC
Chambersburg PA
CBHW050655160426
43194CB00010B/1952